FOR THI

poems for the lovers dismissed by the world.

WRITTEN BY
J. M. WALKER

ILLUSTRATED BY
LYNDA CORTEZ

FOR THE BRAVE ONES
Copyright © 2018 Jude Marie Walker
Illustrations © Lynda Cortez
All rights reserved.

ISBN-13: 978-1982093532
ISBN-10: 198209356

I've written a lot of poems for people
                who didn't deserve them.

That's why today, I chose someone who did.

                Someone who always will.

THE REAL REASON YOU DIDN'T CALL HOME

You found yourself
Slipping, down a street somewhere in Texas
latching on to nothing but sparkling silver eyelids.
You didn't ask her for a smile so kind,
she's offering it to you like a birthday gift
one you never had the courage to ask your parents for.

You weave your hands
in your pockets, playing quiet
while your lungs are screaming
begging, really
for you to inhale something other than caution.
Her fingernails are black
her shirt warm white, soft in summer wind
You don't know what to call her
in your chaotic classifications of humans you've met
so you settle into a sigh
and sit on the street curb
with her
watching the sun dance its worst
across a fire-screaming sky.
If the crows would shut up
maybe you could think
clearer?
She's swirling her Sonic cup
and crunching the ice between her teeth,
now passing the cup to you.
The straw
it has lipstick, red
pink, really
and it's going to touch your lips
the way it touched hers
So you take a sip
kissing the sides of the straw her lipstick stained
and for a moment,
you can breathe.

FOLLOW ME

I think one day
when the sky gets smaller
and the days get longer

I'll kiss you.

I'd like to tiptoe through your thoughts
and play tag with your eyes
You remind me of the hideouts
and wood forts
from scrap wood
I trash picked as a kid
We could make something out of anything.
The way your hands wave furiously when you talk
I know you could build a city
from scratch

I have a feeling you like tree forts too.

Come with me
and I'll show you
the overgrown home I used know
the places my brother and I would go
with stick swords in hand
sweaty palms clutching fate
I'm always captain
but fiiine
this time,
you can be my first mate

                              AWAY! Through sea monster moss
                                    in the silver stone creek
                                            watch your step!
                                            what do you see?

Butterflies
tree hole eyes
caterpillars
huge horse-flies
stones and throws
bows, arrows
shoes or none
feet flying

RUN!
Tickling grass
don't be last
brambles break
you and I
could make
anything
we begin with
nothing
just follow me
this way,

FOLLOW ME!

THE DEFINITION OF TWELVE

If I was twelve
maybe I would believe
that cardboard boxes are rockets and castles
But not penthouses
I didn't really know what those were.

I didn't pay rent,
Rent was what I did with VHS tapes
at the library

Libraries were my churches
and church was fun
when I wore flowers
and sat a little too close to Connor

Connor was a boy
with long pretty hair
and a cheap guitar

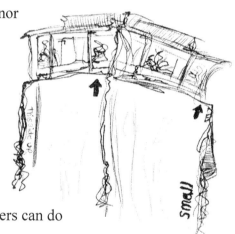

Guitar lessons
were an expensive hobby
I had to drop
after my parents split

Splits are something good dancers can do
Dancers are people
sometimes toothpicks
that do violent things to their feet
and look pretty doing it

That is what I know of being twelve.

DEAR NATALIE,

You were right the first time.

You can always play the prince
when your friends ask to play dress up
You have a vest,
wear it
forget the shirt
feel the sun on your shoulders

Your name is Hero
is Luke Skywalker
is Jim Hawkins
is Robin Hood
every man you've ever been
is alive and well
inside of your chest
let them out again,
you were right the first time.

Love,

Jude

IF LOGIC IS THE PROBLEM

My dad is the most intelligent person I know.

He studies the Riemann Hypothesis on weekends
and marks his calendar for solar eclipses,
counting magnificent meteorites
while the rest of us
wait wide-eyed for "shooting stars"

The Double-Slit Experiment is a Saturday afternoon,
listening acutely while Bohr and Einstein feud
Dad sips unsweet tea
that he sweetened himself

The King's Gambit ignites his chess games
while hopeful opponents fret with pawns, kindling his flames
he hears everything
he listening softly
he watches the world closely for its mathematical stories

He knew me as Natalie,
spent years training his tongue to agree
still after twenty-two years

My dad calls me Jude.

THE LOUDEST LIES

I am too specific of an organism
                              clouded in complexities
                                drowning in doubts
                                  asking too much
                                   by being myself

My name is "social resistance"
My face and frame betray my spirit
My self-expression odd
My style a fad
My voice a sing-song traitor
My anatomy my identity

      Yet a friend once told me

      "Everything you are is tailor made"

           and I heard her sincerity.

So I prayed
that these lies would fade behind the shimmer
of such a soul shining garment

    as my skin, my name, my truth.

I STOPPED TIME ONCE

                        by looking at your lips
                      and watching the way
                   you shaped your words,
         my favorite sound in the world.

ANSWER TO BE DETERMINED

Question:
If I sit here long enough
watching the sun wake up
stirring my apple cider cup
will time stop with me?

Question:
If I moonwalk five years back
into a past
that I thought I knew
everything about
would I smile and laugh,
brushing my hair behind my ears
and my worries behind my back?

Question:
If I wake up next to you tomorrow,
Can you kiss me like that again?

EXPIRATION DATE

Peace comes
                in pieces

Peace cannot be grasped between
           crumbling
                         finger tips.

I want to unscramble the mosaic
of memories that   float   across my   eyelids
      in a heavy   funeral procession.

I want to lock every promise
secret
wish
that spilled from our lips
in a frosted glass jar
and poke careful holes
through the tin foil lid
so that our words
              can continue
                            to breathe.

I want to stare down the reflection
of earnest eyes
that swam in
          our youthful lies.

You promised you would be

                my best friend all my life
                And maybe you meant that,
                        once.

SONNETS TO SOMETHING

When I'm not in love, what will I write for?

The closing creak "goodbye" of the back door
on the way to join the weekday work parade?
The twisting bubbles in the boiling pot
square dancing by the hips of macaroni noodles?
The birds that sing too little and too loud
Crickets with violin legs crackling out of tune
Thunder that forgets to follow the face of lightning
Dogs who honestly forget their names
Recycling bins half full
Garbage cans half empty
The swing of a record player
The sway of a skirt
Painted toe nails
and chipped day dreams

I guess I'm still in love with something.

CHRISTMAS EVE'S EVE

I used to look forward to this day
with many more marks on my calendar
when I was any age
before 13.

One year, someone said it wasn't worth celebrating
But I was 10
and they were wrong.

Every day in December
was worth waking early
to carefully swirl a crisp, red line across the new day's date
and ride down the stairs with all the fanfare I could muster
to announce our newest proximity to Christmas.
(Proximity. A word I did not know at age 4,
but certainly would have liked to.)

Before opening the gates of my bedroom door
(drawbridge and all)
I called to my trusty steed Morgan
who waited patiently in the closet
for me to rise from bed and summon him.

Immediately
the music bellowed around me
alerting all the fairies that slept between my books
to awaken the other animals for our journey down the stairs.
My lions shimmied out from under the bed
My snakes spun out of my sock drawer
All nine of my cats leapt from the uppermost part of my desk
while the doves frantically fluttered from my pillows.
(Pillows. They were quite large to me at age 4,
so none of the doves felt crowded.)

Then began the descent.

The moment the door burst open, drawbridge and all,
the creatures tumbled out into their best formation.
Snakes at the front, cats right behind
Lions drawing up the rear with fairies and doves dancing above.
Morgan and I would stride between the lions and the cats
in our tallest stature with our royal decree:

CHRISTMAS EVE'S EVE TONIGHT,
HEAR ME,
CHRISTMAS EVE'S EVE!

Down the slightly spiraling staircase we would march
until we came upon our loyal audience of one.
My mother waited at the landing,
laughing at my ridiculously wide stance and stoic face.
She did not see my holiday parade
that so eagerly came to greet her.

                                                    "Good morning," she smiled.

THE FIRST THING YOU FORGET

What is there to prove?

You're not just dust,
you're stardust.

You're every shooting star you wished on
every dripping, sparkling
birthday cake candle
Every tooth in an envelope under your pillow
Every penny your grandma gave you
to hurl into the water

All those dandelions you blew apart
are finally taking root
The seeds you planted as a child
are singing back to you.

ON DRINKING SCOTCH AND BEING BRAVE

"Being gay doesn't run in my family, it *gallops!*"
She laughs with all her teeth
and a splash of her drink
as I sip my virgin strawberry daiquiri in teenage jealousy.
She is far beyond my wisdom, my years
my stories, fears, my passport stamps
Yet she chose to sit next to me
at the corner of the bar in our neighborhood Chili's.

I wonder if the word "gay"
has ever been tossed so flamboyantly
into the rhythm of this bar.
She doesn't even pause,
in her true Barbara fashion
She is barreling through the next golden story
to the shining punch line
Her radiant eyes
shaping the story
with so many exclamation points
that her hands feel inclined to orchestrate too
Her silver bracelets swing round and round her wrists
jingling and shimmering center stage.

She is magnificent, everyone knows it
"Another scotch on the rocks!"
and the bartender agrees
This woman is made of steel and stories,
a golden champion of beauty and brilliance.

A photographer once paused us
with a warm "excuse me"
to tell her
she had a movie star's bone structure
like he had never seen
She smiled and said
"Shoulda seen me when I was 19!"

For my beloved friend, Barbara Lauria

IF I WERE BORN A BOY

You would ask to borrow my ties on weekends,
take me out for rounds upon rounds of golf
Clap me on the shoulder
while we sip stouts
and bask in the beauty of our well-paying jobs.

You would love my girlfriend.
You would applaud me for bringing home
such a beautiful, brilliant, interesting woman
to sit with us for Sunday supper
You would hold her hand during the dinner blessing
and squeeze it earnestly after Amen
saying What a fine young lady she was
and beaming What a smart young man I was
and asking What are our plans after graduation?

The evening would be a hum of
Please pass the biscuits
and This gravy is delicious
and I could hold her hand on top of the table
for the family to smile and see.

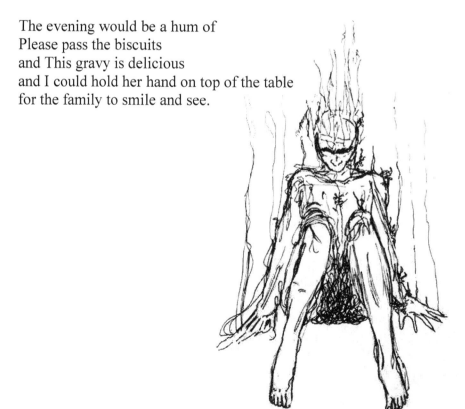

I BOUGHT A BOWTIE

So now
boys compliment
my clothes

because

they wish
they owned them.

I SAW THEM AGAIN

Letting a pair of blades
that close to my face
took 20 years
and a shot of whiskey.

Well, almost.
The recipe wasn't quite that simple,
if I'm completely honest with you

Letting a pair of blades
near the nape of my neck
felt like stripping on the highway
in the middle of February
standing boldly naked
in a circus of oncoming headlights
screaming a name
that had always been mine,
if I'm completely honest with you

Throwing away my training wheels
I tucked behind my ears
Casting off my hideaway
that lovers once brushed away
when they wanted a glimpse
of a girl wrapped in curls,
just a flicker
just a feeling

a girl.

girl?

What do you mean
girl?

The electric razor snaps off and my head is still intact. I think?
The woman responsible for the hair pile graveyard
is nodding approvingly. Shit.
She's done.
She's gonna turn me
around.
I gotta look
in the
mirror now.
Well. This is it.
this is The End
or The Beginning?
or something
dramatic? that I didn't really bargain for this innocent afternoon?
I guess this is what happens when you get too brave, you know.
you end up in a spinny chair with hair all around you
Okay wow that's a lot of hair?
oh God she's turning me
around.
Just keep looking
down?
maybe I'm still there?
maybe it will feel good?
maybe I can just
just maybe it'll look like
well maybe I'll be
okay I'll
just breathe first and

Oh.

Hello.

It's so good to see you again.

THE BALCONY SCENE

I blow kisses

to Jupiter, now

Remembering

your back porch

the concrete steps

the faint smell of spring

the constant inhale of

you.

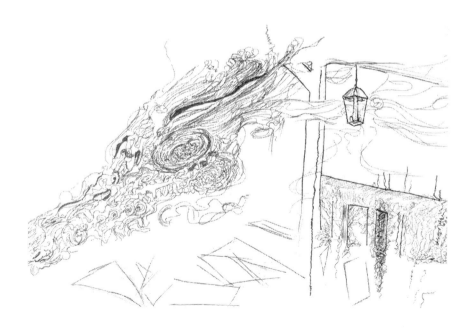

THE DAY THE SKY SPLIT

Do you hear it?

That's not just thunder, it's a stampede.

All your day dreams

you scribbled on scratch paper

in the back of your math class

are racing back to you

They are panting,

joyously

they've been waiting for this day

"Finally," they breathe

"We found you again."

CAN I SHARE SOMETHING WITH YOU?

Every time someone
calls me by my true name

I hear them saying

I love you.

LISTEN,

you will survive by forcing your roots into a soil
that was not laid for you.
Some people just don't desire humans like you
to spread branches across fruitful orchards.
They don't care to share their sun
or share their space
or share their air
because they themselves are scared
of anything stronger
and warmer
and kinder
than they are.

The sound of your silence is exactly what they want.
The people who sleep
between the floor boards of oblivion and fear
do not understand creatures that build homes with their words

Your voice is just as strong as the day you were born
screaming a symphony of sweat and tears
unapologetically
until every single nurse
on every single floor
sang in harmony

THEY LIVE.

BEFORE I THREW OUT YOUR TOOTHBRUSH

I never stopped loving you,
you fell out of love
with me.

The shorter my hair got
the broader my shoulders
the space that swelled around me
seemed too much light
for you to handle

The truth my ears demanded
The mountains I could finally stand in
seemed
to scare you away

Yet I waited
I wanted to be wrong
I waited at the edge
I waited ankle deep in the tide
I delayed my sail

Day after day
waiting for you
to gather up your courage

and love yourself again.

AND STILL THE WIND CHANGES

Bumping down this rambling road I watch the trees twist
and I pray for peace. I watch the clouds churn
and hope for a storm. I look through the cracks of the sky
for the stars I haven't seen yet, the ones pointing out
tomorrow's path. Why do I watch the world with a keener eye
on the days I feel so small?

If all the love I had to give stretched across this road I ride it could
wrap around this shifting city hundreds and hundreds of times.

If my love had arms, it would embrace those that betrayed me
with stern, careful forgiveness.

If my love had lips, it would sing a song of tomorrow,
blowing kisses to yesterday in the kindest way.

If my love had feet, it would run faster than the wind herself,
tangling its hair in the quivering branches as it passed.

But today my love simply has eyes.
It watches the world and prays for signs.

TO THE GIRLS WHO THINK THEY ARE IMPOSSIBLE TO LOVE:

You are not.

I don't care what some locker slamming
hair grazing
dip shit
told you in high school, they were wrong.

Forget the little boys who said you were "too complicated"
but grew up playing with 1,000 piece Lego sets,
they were just scared.

They were raised thinking that they could be anything
except good lovers.
Remember on the playground
how they would push and shove
instead of hug and hold
Because they were told
that "love was for girls"
and "girls were for boys," just whenever boys wanted them.

Don't listen to the exasperated sighs
on the end of the line
when you reach out for help and he simply hangs up
When even the dark dial tone is brighter than his voice
you get to make the choice
to never call back.

This is not your fault.
You are not broken or crazy or toxic
You are stunning and brilliant and a sea of wonder

Some people can't look at the ocean
without getting seasick
so leave him on land,
and crash with your tide.

TO THE GIRLS IN HIDING
WHO DON'T KNOW THEIR BEAUTY:

Sometimes
you must remember
who you were
before the world tried to tell you.

That little girl
riding her bike in her rain boots
on a sunny day, purple cape streaming behind her
while the city stopped to watch you ride
you weren't even five
Remind yourself
how the wind tickled the ribbons of your long wavy hair
how you could cruise down that crowded block
in four minutes flat
without a single stop
The pedestrians watched your pedals spin
jumping abruptly out of your way

You can still fly like that today

You can live at the top again
The top of your heart, lungs, old silver bike
that girl never forgot how to ride
Just because someone told you
to leave your passion in a wasp-ridden garage
spring cleaning has not suddenly become outlawed

Crusade the cobwebs that dirty your dearest memories
No one can tell you that your desires are "stupid fantasies"
Because the fantastical will always seem impractical
to the poor-hearted humans
who stopped believing in their dreams.

HANDSOME

Call me by my jawline
my shoulders
my swayed spine
my knuckles
my growl
my ease
my power
my calves
my feet
my stance
in this street

standing before you,
the human that I am
brushing off
"beautiful"
with a lick of my lips
I am metal and mountains
What?

You've never seen a man like this.

HANG THIS ON THE FRIDGE IF YOU FORGET

Sometimes I see myself
Trapped
in a picture frame
cased in yesterday or

Flat
on a piece of paper
stretched in a strained smile or

Cracked
on a phone screen
with a low battery life or

Stuck
on a fridge door
with a three-legged cat magnet

and ask why the hell it took me so long to cut my damn hair.

THE FAMILY OF PLANETS

A rooftop sunset on a Sunday evening
cherry red toenails painted imperfectly
tiny braids in tangled hair
newborn autumn air

This is what life can always be.
A moment alone with just the trees
and I feel myself sitting firmly
on this earth.
With this face.
With these eyes.

I love my eyes because my eyes are my mother's.
The same eyes as my broad-shouldered brother
Not the youngest one, with the funniest words
improvising life with bicycles and Pokémon cards

Sometimes I miss my family
All the time I miss my family.

I like that quote about how friends are like stars
"when you don't see them
you know they're always there"

Well if friends are stars, families are planets

Constantly
rotating and revolving
with you and around you
pulling you and pushing you
reminding you to

KEEP GOING YOU CAN DO IT
                    or
                    PLEASE GET OUT OF MY ROOM

And even when you don't see them,
you can feel them
moving and shaping your universe
whether you like it or not.

I think I like it

I know I like it

I know I love them.

Together,
we are a universe
of supernovae and newborn stars
inhaling flames
exhaling vibrant light

I wouldn't trade even our darkest of matters
for our longest of light years

They shape and shift my universe,
I'll happily shine for them.

JUST BECAUSE YOU CAN MAKE ME LAUGH,

do not look at me like that
if you have no heart for listening.

I have no patience
for hasty hands
for empty words
for grabbing glances

Do not fill up my glass
if you cannot
sit still by my side
Words were meant
for minds to meet
Not digging holes
for flesh to meld

If ever my skin
desires yours,
You'll know it in your soul
Not your sweaty palms
or famished fingers
So stop reaching.

Ask me of my stories
and lovingly
learn my world.

LAUNDRY DAY

Sometimes I spend my evenings matching socks,
remembering the time I was my mother's right hand man
when it was laundry day

I like putting pairs together
finding patterns, lining up the seams
wrapping the tubes of thread
around one another
so they can keep each other warm
no matter the season

I think my mom taught me to fold
because she believed in love

Hear me out,

Even socks have matches.
Even the little cloth hammocks
we wrap around our ten smelly pigs
are born with a mate
or find one eventually
when laundry day comes.

Sometimes it just isn't laundry day.
Sometimes it's Thursday
and you're wearing mismatched socks.

TELLING MY MOTHER

It was as you might have guessed:
a puddle of tears on the bathroom floor
a summer's day with windows shut
a pair of shaking hands seeking refuge anywhere
anywhere at all
anywhere but here

When I found the words in the back of my throat,
It took every courageous consonant to hold them.
Every flicker of a feeling I had when I was five
every dream or thought I prayed away
by the side of my crumpled blue bed.

When I sat on that bathroom floor,
I saw who was watching me.
A little hero who loved all the world
in a red and black vest
with a fighter's song in their eyes.

    "Today,"

       they said

"Today you tell her who I am."

GROWING PAINS

As I developed new calluses playing guitar,

I welcomed new skin

to my fingers and palms

Learning the power

of being soft as steel.

THE LIST

My childhood room
feels like a museum
no matter how many times
I dust the shelves.

The books are still my pride and joy
but their covers haven't been caressed in
years?

Has it really been
years?

I light a candle and cradle my thoughts in my cranium
 tapping
        my toes
                in tandem
(with)
     the terrible
          squeak
               in my ceiling fan

I asked my mom to get that fixed
Does she forget these things when I'm not home?
do the doors go unlocked when I'm not home
do the cats go unfed
does the truth go unsaid?
why
do I
no longer
fit
my
child
hood
bed

In the silence, I hear a voice.

Natalie
the little one with the long braided hair
asking Mama for a book for Christmas.

This Christmas, my list consisted of things
no one could seem to buy

This year I asked for peace
I asked for a stable career after college
For a meaningful relationship
that doesn't breed in the dark cracks of insecurity and small talk.

I asked for love
I asked for bathroom mirrors to stop insulting me
For people at grocery stores to smile more.
I asked for patience
I asked for the sun to show her face a little longer
so I could finish everything I promised I would do.
I asked for joy
I asked for rainfall I could dance in
For a snowstorm I could swirl snow angels within
not caring about the ice that might slide up my sleeve.
I asked for knowledge
I asked for the stories of the unheard to be shouted
from skyscrapers
For "politicians" to stop screaming.
I asked for trust
I asked for lying to be illegal
For people to feel safe
when they hold out their hearts in front of them
to another human's touch.

I asked for a new name.
I asked for the courage to remind people who I am.
I asked for a world where I can squeeze the hand
of the human I love
without a sideways glance.

I WAS TOO IN LOVE WITH THE WORLD   TO BE IN LOVE WITH JUST YOU.

I know it's technically "after noon" because it is 12:38pm on the microwave clock, but it still feels like morning. I angle my chair to face the window. If I look through the smudged glass too long I forget how old I am. I feel 11 again, waiting for my best friend to knock at the door so we can take our neighborhood by storm. The boy with the blonde hair that looks like morning and smells like treehouses. All the sweat, dirt and sawdust that met his shirts knew my nose just as well.

We talked about getting married. It was just common sense.
We were 11. We were best friends. I trusted him with more secrets than my lock and key diary. He was the only one who didn't look at me funny when I asked to play pirates.
He would paint me swords instead.

I still see him on holidays
or weekends
or train stops
between seasons

He's at my front door with the sun in his hair.
He's complimenting my new hair cut because it "makes me look like a ninja." He's handing me the swords he painted just for me. Blue and silver. I was the blue and silver hero.

HEART OVER HANDS

Thank you
for sitting with me
on top of the parking garage
in our persistent winter
and letting my eyes drift
away from yours.
Thank you
for listening
with both ears
and no hands
because too many people
have my love language wrong.
You offered to hug me
without clasping your hands
around my ribs too tight
so I knew you meant it.
You understood what I meant
when I said
hungry hands scare me

so you offered me words
and a heart instead.

RESILIENCE

I will tell you what beauty is on your worst day.

I can rewrite curses into sonnets

by staring at them

and tilting my head

ever
so
slightly.

I believe that spring comes strong

after every winter

and if I do not see the sunrise,

I thank her for the view all the same

I think endings can be poignant

beginnings can be poetry

bruises can tell stories

and scars can sing melodies

I wear my brightest eyes

on the rainiest days

I can find the window in the basement

and the clover in the weeds

So do not tell me I am stupid

when I say

I will love again.

REVELRY

Keep up with me,
I dare you.

Learn what it's like to live between adventures and aspirations
playing cards with chaos
and sweet talking the moon
But look closely,
she likes me more than you.

Touch the grey streaks the sky yawns before the sun
Dismiss the morning with me,
it would be too dangerous
to welcome her face to face
because

If you watch too many sunrises with someone
you might begin to wake
twisting your sheets in smiles,
whispering their name.

FOR THE BRAVE ONES

I still believe in love because I can feel it.

Though humans have a talent for forgetting one another
there will always be those
with courage in their kisses
with softness in their shoulders
sometimes even with matching socks
We are the ones
who refuse to run.

We don't dismiss fairy tales as child's play,
we know children have more wisdom than many believe
we don't call such stories "tales,"
we call them miracles.

We still believe in love because we see it in our sky.

We see each sunset as an opportunity
for a new exhale of stars across a darkened, tired blue
We see our world come back to life every night
between the last wishes of dying stars
and the steady heartbeats of the youngest ones.

We know that constellations are just soul mates,
stars that finally found each other
after billions of burning years
fuming for the moment they could glow together

And yet
maybe our moment is not today?

Maybe we're tired of feeling nothing but fire,
watching the sunset with a blazing sense of urgency
Maybe we've done nothing but shine our whole lives
praying that our light will lead someone home to us

And yet
we do not cease flying through the sky,
all hope and heart as if we were born to do so.

Before telescopes, before star charts
before Galileo, Copernicus
and the curious that observed us
We knew that love was bigger
than oceans and land
that our earth may be beautiful
but cannot withstand
the fire and rock
that shapes who we are

Because us brave ones,
who still believe in love,

                we are the stars.

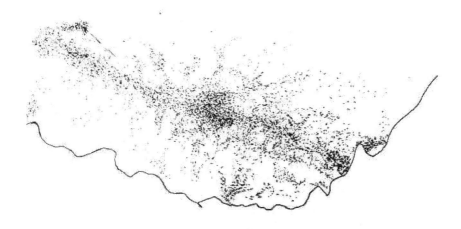

ACKNOWLEDGEMENTS

This little piece of heart finally exists in print thanks to the encouragement and counsel of Mason Conrad, Bruce Longworth, Suzanne Mills, Trace Turner, Cathy Hutchison and the small but mighty Webster Poetry Club. Special thanks to Lynda Cortez for being the best collaborator, artist and partner-in-crime
a person could ever ask for.

A sea of love and gratitude to Cheryl, Mitch, Major, Silas, Hudson and Lorena for their inspiration and love. Thank you for loving me no matter what my name was, is and will be.

A special thank you to the curious readers who made it this far. Your patience and compassion mean the world to me, even if you do not understand these stories.

A storm of courage and strength to the brave ones who know these stories all too well. Our Creator did not make a mistake when you were created. Never forget that. Your light is contagious.
This book belongs to you.

ABOUT THE AUTHOR

Jude Walker is a non-binary actor and a writer who spent most of their childhood playing pirates and building forts in Carrollton, Texas. Jude recently graduated from the Webster Conservatory of Theatre Arts in St. Louis, where they earned their BFA in Acting and Minor in Business. Jude asks politely that you please purchase this little book so that they can pay off their student loans and buy their Mom a beach house.

ABOUT THE ILLUSTRATOR

Lynda Cortez is an artist/student hailing from New Orleans. They currently attend the Webster Conservatory of Theatre Arts for acting, but you may also find them sketching at the park or dancing and singing eccentrically in the streets. Lynda would like to thank their mom for her unconditional support in whatever they do.

Made in the
USA
Lexington, KY